HIPAA Compliance

For

Healthcare Administrative Professionals

By

Martha E. Sims Rodriguez BS. CPC.

Publisher: Health Tec Systems

1

Disclaimer

Attempts have been made to provide current accurate information.

Readers are encouraged to verify facts with the related industry reference materials.

No guarantee is made. Readers are encouraged to verify all information.

Please read the following:

Reader agrees that Health Tec Systems and its employees and agents shall not

be held responsible or liable for any actions taken by Client, or

any error, inaccuracy, or omission in any report or analysis Client prepares in connection with or through use of this training material nor, any damage (including, but not limited to consequential damages) resulting from it.

CPT codes are published by the American Medical Association and are used in this lesson with the intent of educating the reader. ICD 10 are published by the World Health Organization.

Contents

Dedication

This book is dedicated to my wonderful former students.

Especially those in California. Many of them have successful careers in the healthcare industry helping patients and their families.

Foreword

Course participants will learn the most recent Details of the Health Insurance Portability Accountability Act passed by Congress. This course will simplify the administrative components of the act.

While taking this course you may want to complete the retention quiz at the end of the book. You may also take the online quiz where there is an achievement certificate available once obtaining a passing score of 70% or better.

Many industry resources will be referenced. The information will assist medical providers, insurance carrier professionals understand mandated regulations so that they may be in Compliance.

The course will cover history and implementation requirements.

The most recent HIPAA regulations are reviewed including but not limited to:

* Privacy Standards

* Security Standards

* Uniform Identifier Standards

* Transaction and Code Set Standards

HIPAA legislation went into effect in 1996. We are past the implementation phase of HIPAA and currently HIPAA is in the "Enforcement stage".

Congratulations on your reading this book.

The learning out-comes are for you and your staff to be up-to- date on mandated HIPAA legislation.

In a lecture I once heard an attorney state

"The best way to avoid a government or payer audit is to have a Compliance Program in place."

Why HIPAA Training?

HIPAA regulations require any HIPAA covered entity are required to train all members of its workforce. This training must include the practice's policies and procedures with respect to PHI (Protected Health Information). The training has to include how to handle confidential information per your company policies and procedures.

Company policies and procedures create safeguards for administrative, technical and physical safeguards used to keep PHI reasonably safe, keeping PHI from use or disclosure that violates HIPAA.

Examples of safeguards

Administrative

- Requiring identification of an individual picking up health records
- Asking for a written release of records from a 3rd party copying service.
- Signed business associate agreement on file for vendors or contracted services staff.

Technical

- Patient sign-in sheets limit information requested and are change periodically during the day.
- Acknowledgment of receipt signed by patient about practice privacy practices. Or attempt to get signed forms documented in the patient's medical record.
- Keep computer screen turned so that viewing is restricted to authorized personnel.
- Username and passwords are kept confidential and changed often.

Physical

- Fax machines should be placed where only staff members have access.
- Send all privacy-related questions or concerns to appropriate staff member.
- Immediately report any suspected or known improper behavior to supervisor or compliance officer.

Who Over Sees HIPAA

Delegation of Authority To Administer the Health Insurance Portability and Accountability Act of 1996 Security Rule

On October 7, 2003, HHS delegated to the Centers for Medicare & Medicaid Services (CMS) the

authority to enforce compliance with the Security Rule and to impose civil monetary penalties on covered entities that violate it. The Final Rule for enforcement of the Security Rule became

effective on March 16, 2006 (71 Fed. Reg. 8390 (Feb. 16, 2006)).

On July 27, 2009, HHS delegated the authority for the oversight and enforcement of the Security

Rule to the Office for Civil Rights (OCR).

Responsibilities of the Office for Civil Rights
As HHS's civil rights, health information privacy, and security enforcement division, OCR's purpose is to protect fundamental rights of nondiscrimination and ensure compliance with health
information privacy and security laws. As of July 27, 2009, OCR became responsible for ensuring that covered entities comply with the Security Rule and for investigating and resolving potential HIPAA violations.

IT Security Checklist

Implement the security controls in the information system. NIST SP 800-70, Security Configuration Checklists Program for IT Products, presents information about security configuration checklists and their

benefits, and explains how to use the NIST Checklist Program to find and retrieve checklists. Checklists of security settings are useful tools that have been developed to guide IT administrators and security personnel in selecting effective security settings that will reduce the risks and protect systems from attacks. Checklists can be effective in reducing vulnerabilities to systems, especially for small organizations with
limited resources. IT vendors often create checklists for their own products, but other organizations such as consortia, academic groups, and government agencies have also developed them. Information about the NIST Checklists Program is available from
http://checklists.nist.gov/.

Have you conducted the following six required annual Audits/Assessments?

☐

Use the checkboxes below to self-evaluate HIPAA compliance in your practice or organization.
Security Risk Assessment

Required Annual Audits/Assessments

Privacy Standards Audit (Not required

for BAs)
HITECH Subtitle D Privacy Audit
Security Standards Audit
Asset And Device Audit
Physical Site Audit
Have You Documented All
Deficiencies?

☐ Documenting Gaps

Have you created remediation plans to
address deficiencies found in all six
Audits?

☐ remediation plans

Are these remediation plans fully
documented in writing?
Do you update and review these
remediation plans annually?
re annually documented remediation
plans retained in your records for six

years?

Have you identified all gaps uncovered in the audits above?

AUDIT TIP: If audited, you must provide all documentation
for the past six years to auditors.

☐ Have all staff members undergone annual HIPAA training?

☐

Staff Training

Do you have documentation of their training?

Is there a staff member designated as the HIPAA Compliance, Privacy, and/or Security Officer?

Have all staff members read and

legally attested to the Policies and Procedures?

Policies and Procedures vendors and business associates

Have you identified all of your vendors and Business Associates?

Do you have Business Associate Agreements in place with all Business Associates?

Do you have Policies and Procedures relevant to the annual HIPAA Privacy, Security, and Breach Notification Rules?

Do you have documentation for annual reviews of your Policies and Procedures?

Do you have documentation of their legal attestation?

Have you performed due diligence on your Business Associates to assess their HIPAA compliance?

Are you tracking and reviewing your Business Associate Agreements annually?

Do you have Confidentiality Agreements with non-Business Associate vendors?

Do you have a defined process for incidents or breaches?

Breaches

Do you have the ability to track and manage the investigations of all incidents?

Are you able to provide the required reporting of minor or meaningful breaches
or incidents?

Do your staff members have the ability to anonymously report an incident?

Reasons to Comply

Healthcare breaches lead the way
Patient records are 44 percent of all documents compromised

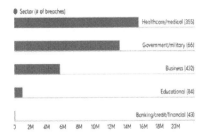

● Sector (# of breaches)

	Healthcare/medical (355)
	Government/military (66)
	Business (432)
	Educational (84)
	Banking/credit/financial (43)

0   2M   4M   6M   8M   10M   12M   14M   16M   18M   20M

Source: Identity Theft Resource Center, 2016 data

Who Must Comply with HIPAA?

HIPAA Regulations must be followed by:

- **Clearinghouses**
  - (example: Health Care Billing Companies)
- **Health Plans**
  - (example: Blue Cross/Blue Shield Health Insurance, Dental or Optical Insurance Plans)
- **Providers**
  - (example: Hospitals, Pharmacies, Physician Offices, Ambulance Companies, Durable Medical Equipment etc)
  - *Anyone who maintains or transmits health information electronically*

23

Penalties for Non-Compliance of HIPAA

What are the penalties for violating HIPAA?

Culpability	Minimum Penalty per	Maximum Penalty per

	Violation [1]	Violation[2]
1. No Knowledge	$100	$50,000
2. Reasonable cause	$1,000	$50,000
3. Willful neglect, timely corrected	$10,000	$50,000
4. Willful neglect, not timely	$50,000	$50,000

The offenses are per a violation. The per violation is estimated using extrapolation.

If 10 charts were evaluation for an audit and 2 of them had a violation issue.

The extrapolation would suggest that 20% of the charts are in violation.

Enforcement Results by State

The table below represents the enforcement resolutions pertaining to complaints received, for each state for the period from April 14, 2003 through December 31, 2021.

There were:

STATE	INVESTIGATED: NO VIOLATION	RESOLVED AFTER INTAKE AND REVIEW	INVESTIGATED: CORRECTIVE ACTION
AK	5%	66%	29%
AL	5%	70%	26%
AR	7%	67%	26%
AZ	4%	66%	30%
CA	4%	71%	25%
CO	5%	68%	27%
CT	7%	67%	26%

STATE	INVESTIGATED: NO VIOLATION	RESOLVED AFTER INTAKE AND REVIEW	INVESTIGATED: CORRECTIVE ACTION
DC	5%	70%	24%
DE	7%	65%	28%
FL	4%	68%	27%
GA	4%	70%	26%
HI	3%	69%	28%
IA	3%	74%	23%
ID	4%	68%	28%
IL	5%	67%	28%
IN	5%	70%	25%
KS	4%	73%	23%
KY	5%	71%	24%
LA	5%	70%	25%

STATE	INVESTIGATED: NO VIOLATION	RESOLVED AFTER INTAKE AND REVIEW	INVESTIGATED: CORRECTIVE ACTION
MA	8%	63%	29%
MD	6%	65%	29%
ME	8%	67%	24%
MI	5%	69%	26%
MN	4%	70%	26%
MO	4%	70%	26%
MS	5%	73%	22%
MT	7%	70%	23%
NC	5%	68%	27%
ND	7%	67%	26%
NE	3%	75%	22%
NH	8%	65%	28%

STATE	INVESTIGATED: NO VIOLATION	RESOLVED AFTER INTAKE AND REVIEW	INVESTIGATED: CORRECTIVE ACTION
NJ	4%	67%	29%
NM	5%	68%	27%
NV	3%	72%	25%
NY	4%	70%	26%
OH	4%	69%	27%
OK	6%	67%	27%
OR	4%	68%	28%
PA	6%	67%	27%
RI	11%	54%	36%
SC	5%	69%	27%
SD	6%	68%	26%
TN	5%	68%	28%

STATE	INVESTIGATED: NO VIOLATION	RESOLVED AFTER INTAKE AND REVIEW	INVESTIGATED: CORRECTIVE ACTION
TX	5%	69%	26%
UT	5%	68%	27%
VA	6%	67%	27%
VT	8%	69%	24%
WA	4%	67%	30%
WI	5%	68%	27%
WV	7%	71%	22%
WY	6%	66%	27%

Resources: For Current Regulations

Federal Register:

https://www.govinfo.gov/content/pkg/FR-2013-01-25/pdf/2013-01073.pdf

•American Dental Association
website: http://www.ada.org/goto/hipaa.
•AADS (charts and forms) website:
http:www.aads.com.
•National Dental EDI Council
website: http://www.ndedic.org/.
•US Department of Health and Human Services
website: http://aspe.os.dhhs.gov/admnsimp/.
•Health Tec Systems
Website: http://www.healthtecsystems

.com

Privacy Rule

- How health Information is used and stored.

    The health provider must disclose if they are participating in research, or advertising.

    If the patient refuses to sign the Privacy Notice.
    The Healthcare provider should document that and effort to get an signature of approval, however it was declined.

    The law dose not prohibit use of the patient info, if not signed.
    In all cases patients must be notified when info will be used.

33

Five Main Parts HIPAA

- Privacy Rule
- Security Rule
- Transactions and code Sets
- Uniform identifier standards
- Enforcement Rule

Security Rule

This rule addresses the physical storage and transmission of patient data.

Computer systems must have passwords, use logs, encryption for electronic transmission such as insurance verification and billing.

Policies and procedures must be in place as well of how and where servers and computers should be housed.

Transactions and code Sets

Insurance billing standard billing practices.
Such as CMS 1500 form for professional provider billing and
  UB 04 for Hospital Billing.
ADA = ADA form and codes
Coding DX = ICD 10
Procedures = CPT or HCPCS
Procedure coding inpatient = ICD 10 PCS
Employers = EIN
Providers = NPI

Working the Plan

Step 1: Develop a Written Policy

Your written policy or plan should describe how you and your team will meet HIPAA compliance criteria and how PHI will be evaluated and monitored as it is obtained and provided by your office.

Contact

FOLLOW-UP COMPLIANCE

Step 2: Assign A Privacy Officer and Contact Person

Identify an individual who can be accountable for overseeing operations as your Privacy Officer. This individual should have a genuine interest in patient privacy. Of equal importance, they should be well organized, articulate, and willing to accept responsibility for supervision of compliance. The Privacy Officer would receive patient requests for obtaining access to their PHI or requesting an amendment to their PHI.

38

The officer would be responsible for maintaining records for complaints and can act as (or appoint) a Contact Person to receive complaints. If the Privacy Officer shares the role of the Contact Person, then they must also be professionally mature and non-emotional. This is of particular importance when dealing with patient-related complaints.

Step 3: Team Training

Training is a very important aspect of HIPAA compliance. HIPAA requires that all employers and employees alike are provided training on HIPAA compliance by April 14, 2003, in Privacy Etiquette. If an employee violates compliance requirements, an incident report is to be filed, and disciplinary action should follow to ensure that the behavior is not repeated.

Patients Rights

- Be informed of the organization's privacy practices by receiving notice of Privacy Practices (NPP).
- Have their information kept confidential and secure
- Be informed it their information will be used in advertisement or research.
- Obtain a copy of their health record (a small fee may apply).
- Request to have their health records amended.
- Request special considerations in communication.
- Restrict unauthorized access to their confidential health information.

General Use of Written Acknowledgement and Authorization Forms

Most providers are familiar with the *Federal Register* mandates.

They are aware that after providing the patient with the NPP (Notice of Privacy Practices.) If the patient refuses to sign or is unable to sign, this must be documented in the patient record.

Authorization forms this is protection for the practice. Providers must know and understand the forms used in their office. Pscychotherapy notes are handled separately under HIPAA. Such notes have additional protection, specifically, that an authorization for any use of disclosure of psychotherapy notes must be obtained.

Provider organizations are expected to handle requests made by patients to exercise their rights.

There should be an office policy on dealing with each specific request. The policy would be specific to you health care practice.

The patients cannot keep their confidential health information from being used for treatment, payment (unless they are paying the bill)

Or healthcare operations nor may they force amendments to their health record.

Most agreements are good for one year and should be renewed.

If this is in your policies, it offers a great time to update demographic information on the patients.

Step 4: Business Associate Safeguards

All business associates (BA) (a person or entity that performs or assists in the performance of a function or activity involving the use or disclosure of PHI, such as accountants, consultants, financial institutions, management consultants, advisors, computer software vendors, answering services, dental laboratories, and temporary employees) must provide healthcare providers safeguards that ensure PHI will not be abused or used for anything other than treatment payment or operational services (TPO).

BAA

- Employees and associates are not included, since they are members of your workforce.
  This requirement can be met through a signed agreement with all BAs. Agreements must be signed by April 14, 2003. The agreement must stipulate that the BA is willing to "open the books" to Health and Human Services (HHS) if privacy has been suspected to be violated.

HIPAA

- ## Step 5: Posting of HIPAA Privacy Policy
  All healthcare providers must post their HIPAA Privacy Policy Notice in a conspicuous place for patient viewing.

- ## Step 6: Patient Acknowledgement of Privacy Policy
  HIPAA requires healthcare providers to obtain patient acknowledgement (acceptance is not required, only acknowledgement) of the healthcare provider's privacy policy. This requirement can be met by having each patient simply acknowledge receiving a copy of the written privacy policy by signing off to that effect. If the patient refuses, a note must be made in the patient's record to indicate the refusal.

47

Step 7: Self Audits

Periodically, healthcare providers need to perform self audits. If at any time the healthcare provider or representatives find any violations, they are to be mitigated as soon as possible to limit further harm to PHI.

HIPAA Compliance

Step 8: Authorization and Record Keeping Logs for Use of PHI for Other Than TPO

In the event that a healthcare provider intends to use PHI for anything other than TPO (Treatment, Payment or Operational Services), the healthcare provider is required to obtain patient authorization. In addition, the healthcare provider is also required to keep a log that discloses who used the information, how it was used, and why it was used. The log, along with authorizations, are to be kept on file for 6 years from the time of use and/or authorization.

Enforcement

Step 9

- Detecting offences
- Responding
- Developing corrective action
- Reporting

Disaster plan

BUSINESS

- Back-up and storage
- Record retrieval
- Emergency operations

PERSONAL

A disaster plan is not mandated by HIPAA but it is highly suggested your practice have one in place.

Seven Basic Components of a Compliance Plan

1. Conducting internal monitoring and auditing.
2. Implementing compliance and practice standards.
3. Designating a compliance officer or contact.
4. Conducting appropriate training and education.
5. Responding appropriately to detected offenses and developing corrective action.
6. Developing open lines of communication.
7. Enforcing disciplinary standards through well-publicized guidelines.
   - Verbal warning
   - Written warning
   - Written reprimand
   - Suspension or probation
   - Demotion
   - Termination of employment
   - Restitution of any damages
   - Referral to federal agencies for criminal prosecution

Take aways from this lesson:

Although every healthcare practice is different, and their policies and procedures will vary each should know what is expected in the workplace:

QUIZ You may access the quiz online, take the quiz and receive a certificate for passing scores. Or you may want to take the quiz here while reading this lesson.

Visit www.HealthTecSystems.com For HIPAA and compliance information.

Quiz

Test: HIPAA 101 for Covered Entities

Name: _____

Date: _____ **Score:**
_____

Question 1

What does the abbreviation HIPAA stand for?

○A) Health Information Protection Accountability Act
○B) Health Insurance Portability and Accountability Act
○C) Health Insurance Protection and Accessibility Act
○D) Healthcare Insurance Portability and Accountability Act Law

Question 2

What year did HIPAA Legislation start?

A)2003
B)2006
C)1996
D)2012

Question 3

What are the 5 HIPAA Rules?

A) Access, Standard Code Transactions, Security, Enforcement, Compliance

B) Security, Privacy, Transactions Standards, Enforcement, Unique Identifiers.

C) Code unification, Employer ID, Security, Privacy, Enforcement

D)Privacy, Security, Transaction Standards, Access, NPI

E) None of the above.

Question 4

OCR is the Abbreviation for Office of Civil Rights

○A)True
○B)False

Question 5

DHHS is the abbreviation for? Department of Health and Human Services.

○A)True
○B)False

Question 6

Medicare is over seen by CMS? Center for Medicare and Medicaid Services?

○A)True
○B)False

Question 7

Should a covered entity require liability insurance of a
business associate?

A)True
B)False

Question 8

Having a compliance program in place is the best way to
avoid an audit?

A)True
B)False

Question 9

How often should rules be reviewed?

○ A)Never, once set into place.
○ B)Weekly
○ C)monthly at a minimum.
○ D)Annually

Question 10

Conducting internal monitoring and auditing is mandatory for having a compliance program in place.

○ A)True
○ B)False

Made in the USA
Middletown, DE
19 September 2023